SUPER MACHINES

John Freeman

Macdonald Educational

How to use this book

First, look at the contents page opposite. Read the chapter list to see if it includes the subject you want. The list tells you what each page is about. You can then find the page with the information you need.

If you want to know about one particular thing, look it up in the index on page 31. For example, if you want to know about forges, the index tells you that there is something about them on pages 26 and 27. The index also lists the pictures in the book.

When you read this book, you will find some unusual words. The glossary on page 30 explains what they mean.

Series Editor
Margaret Conroy

Book Editor
Peter Harrison

Production
Susan Mead

Picture Research
Kathy Lockley

Factual Adviser
Aubrey Tulley

Reading Consultant
Amy Gibbs
Inner London Education Authority
Centre for Language in Primary
Education

Series Design
Robert Mathias/Anne Isseyegh

Book Design
Julia Osorno/Anne Isseyegh

Teacher Panel
Steve Harley
Anne Merriman
Jenny Mules

Illustrations
Mike Atkinson 7,9,10-11,14-15,22-23
Gerard Browne 12-13,21,27,29
Kevin Maddison 10, 12, 16-17, 20, 24-25

Photographs
Cover: a strip mining machine in
Germany

Courtesy BP: 18
BPCC/Aldus Archive: 19
Courtesy British Steel: 26
Earthscan/P. Charlesworth: 23/
M. Edwards, 15
Robert Harding/Griffiths: 21
Hutchison Picture Library: 13
Kew Bridge Engine Trust/P. Wilson: 28
S.N.C.F./Couchat: 6-7
ZEFA/Damm: 25/Freytag 11/Pfaff 8, 16

CONTENTS

MOVING   6-15
Trains   6-7
Shuttle transporter   8-9
Helicopters   10-11
Oil tanker   12-13
Road train   14-15

GATHERING   16-23
Strip mining   16-17
Oil rig   18-19
Combine harvester   20-21
Factory ship   22-23

MAKING   24-29
Tower crane   24-25
Forging metal   26-27
Beam engine   28-29

GLOSSARY, BOOKS TO READ   30

INDEX   31

MOVING

Trains

People have used machines for thousands of years. Although some machines have always been much larger or faster than others, it is only in the last 150 years or so that truly super machines have been built. The first part of this book describes some super moving machines that are faster, or can carry bigger loads, than ever before. The first two examples are trains.

Stephenson's 'Rocket' is named after George Stephenson who won a prize for it in 1829 because it was one of the first locomotives to pull passenger trains. It could travel at nearly 40 kilometres per hour and could pull several trucks or carriages. The carriages were often open-topped, and passengers were sometimes covered by smoke.

Steam moved the 'Rocket'. Water was heated in the boiler until it turned into steam. Then the steam expanded in the cylinders, and pushed on the pistons. These in turn pushed the wheels.

This test model of the Train à très Grande Vitesse is checking that the pantograph which picks up the power from the cables works when the TGV travels at high speed.

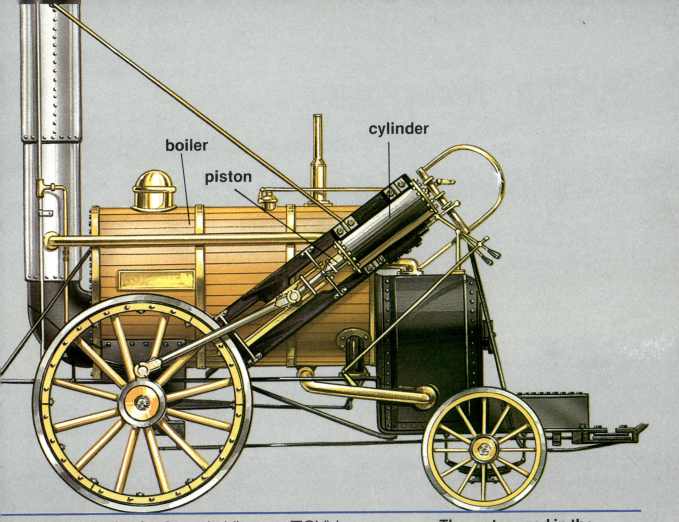

boiler

piston

cylinder

The Train à très Grande Vitesse (TGV) is a modern French supertrain. It travels on specially built track, and carries several hundred passengers in air conditioned coaches at speeds of up to 260 kilometres per hour. Electricity drives the TGV. At top speed, it uses as much as 2100 electric kettles!

The water used in the Rocket's boiler was carried in a tender behind the engine.

Shuttle transporter

Moving machines can be put into the 'super' class for other reasons: for example, when the machine carries a very large load.

The NASA Space Shuttle has attracted attention all over the world, but it is not the only NASA super machine. A tractor-crawler moves the Shuttle from its Vehicle Assembly Building, where the Shuttle is attached to its booster rockets, to the launch pad. It is the biggest road-going vehicle in the world. It weighs 500 tonnes, travels at a maximum speed of 5 kilometres per hour, and has 20 caterpillar tracks, each of them more than three metres high.

The caterpillar tracks on this mining machine are almost the same size as those on the shuttle transporter. They make a person look very small!

The engines which power the tractor-crawler's huge caterpillar tracks are no more powerful than those in an ordinary lorry or truck. This is because although the load is so large, it must be moved very slowly indeed.The Shuttle itself is almost 60 metres tall. If the transporter moved quickly, it could make the Shuttle move from side to side, and possibly cause it to fall over. This would be a disaster.

The road sinks by as much as 15 centimetres as the transporter passes carrying the 2000 tonne Shuttle. Any normal road would break up under this weight. The road which the transporter travels on is specially designed to bend back like a spring after the transporter has moved on.

These huge caterpillar tracks spread out weight because they are so wide. Wheels are narrow, and can carry much less weight.

Helicopters

Helicopters can carry loads to places which no car or lorry could reach. People and machinery can only go by air to some places where there are no roads. Aeroplanes need a runway to land and take off. If there is no runway, aeroplanes can only drop small loads by parachute.

Helicopters are used to fly in larger loads or to pick up cargo because they can land in a small space. They are also often used in rescue operations to reach injured people quickly.

As the blades of the rotor spin round they can also twist up and down slightly. The pilot steers the helicopter by controlling how the blades twist.

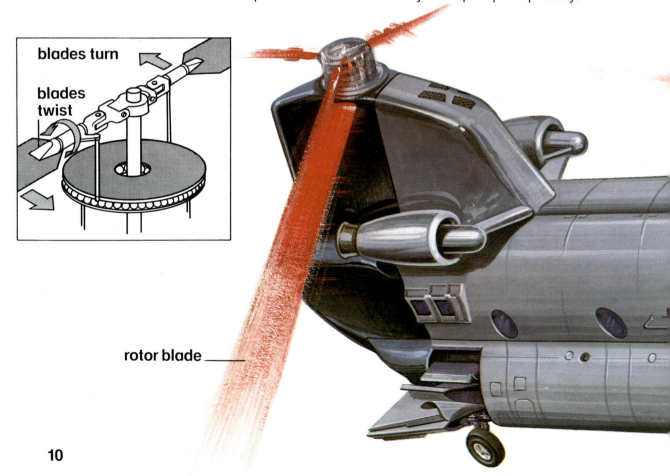

blades turn

blades twist

rotor blade

Although they carry a similar size of load, 'flying crane' helicopters are much more expensive than lorries. They are not used unless large objects need to be carried to places which are hard to reach by any other way. For example, if a remote lighthouse needs spare machinery, or if a ship has broken down at sea, only a helicopter can help quickly.

Large helicopters have two three-bladed rotors that are powered by jet engines. Armies and navies use these kinds of helicopters for landing supplies quickly from ships, and for moving troops.

This flying crane has had most of its body removed to make it lighter, and allow it to carry large loads.

rotor _____

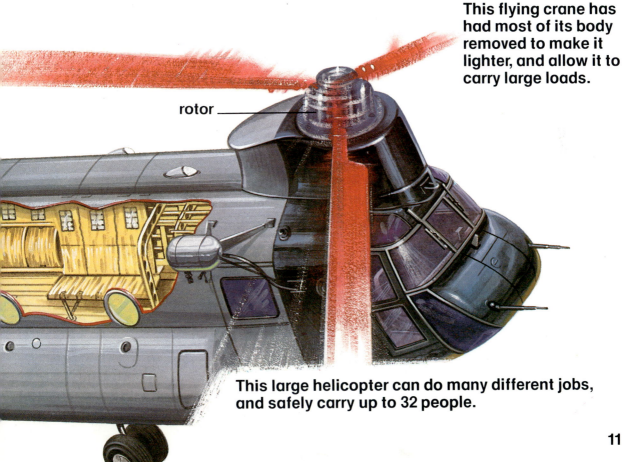

This large helicopter can do many different jobs, and safely carry up to 32 people.

Oil tanker

Modern industry uses many products which are made out of oil, such as gas and petrol. The oil has to travel long distances, because it has to be refined before it can be turned into different products.

Special ships called oil tankers carry the oil from the countries where it is found, to refineries in other countries. Because so much oil is needed, it is cheaper to carry it in the largest tankers possible. These are called super-tankers.

Super-tankers can carry 400,000 tonnes of oil, enough to fill more than 250 swimming pools. Since a super-tanker weighs so much, it may travel 5 kilometres before it can stop. This means that the crew must always be careful to look out for other ships in their path. If a super-tanker gets too close to another ship, it might not be able to avoid hitting it.

The oil is stored in several separate tanks beneath the deck, so that if there is a collision, there is a chance that only one tank will be damaged. If oil is spilt on the sea, it can kill many birds and fish.

Using a bicycle for getting around on board an oil tanker. It's quicker than walking!

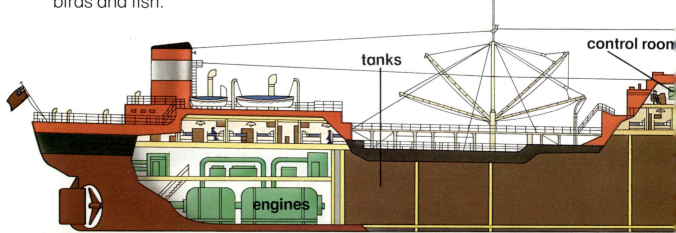

tanks

control room

engines

A tanker leaving Lagos, an oil port in Nigeria.

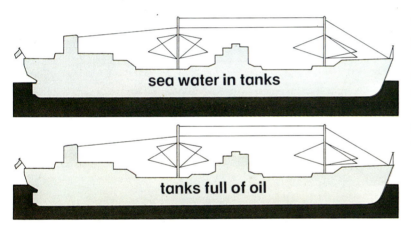

sea water in tanks

tanks full of oil

When there is no oil in the tanks, sea water is put into them to stop the tanker rising too high in the water. When the tanks are full of oil, the tanker lies very low in the water.

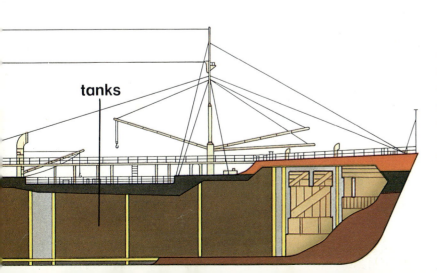

tanks

An oil tanker's engines and propeller are controlled from the middle of the ship. The oil is kept in tanks which are separated by metal walls.

13

Road train

The road train is not a real train, but a large lorry with several trailers which is able to travel on very bumpy roads. Huge countries like Australia or the USA have lots of open country outside the towns. Here, roads are difficult and costly to repair, and the road surfaces are often bad. Goods have to be sent along these roads thousands of kilometres away from farms and factories to the shops.

Drivers have a bed and a kitchen in the cabs of the road trains because their journey may take several weeks. They also have a two-way radio so that they can call for help. Road trains are too large to drive in towns. When they reach their destination, the goods they carry have to be unloaded on to smaller lorries which can drive in city streets.

This road train is carrying a load to a town many kilometres from a railway.

Road trains can carry loads as heavy as 100 tonnes, and they sometimes have as many as 22 wheels. A machine like this costs a lot, perhaps as much as 20 cars! Road trains can travel as fast as 80 kilometres per hour, but may only reach 50 kilometres per hour on bumpy roads far out in open country.

Camel power moves bales of cotton to market in India. The rubber wheels on the cart help it to travel more smoothly.

GATHERING

Strip mining

There are other super machines which can gather harvests of useful material from the earth. When coal or ore is near the surface of the earth we can dig it out without having to sink a mineshaft. This way of mining is called strip mining because the coal is dug out in strips. The mines are usually covered with earth when all the coal has been taken out.

The biggest mobile strip mining machine in the world is called a Bucyrus-Erie 4250W. It is used to mine coal in North America. It weighs 12,000 tonnes, as much as several hundred fully-loaded heavy lorries. The buckets can pick up 500 tonnes of coal, enough to supply a coal fire for about 20 years. The boom is 94.4 metres long.

This is a view of a whole strip mine. The giant machine in the centre has cut the earth away in layers. This is also known as 'open-cast' mining.

If a machine like the Bucyrus-Erie worked for 25 years, it would move about 1000 million cubic metres of rock and coal. If all this were coal, it would make a mountain over 1 kilometre high. The 4250W only needs 20 people to keep it working. It would take 10,000 people with spades and wheelbarrows to mine as much coal as it can. Coal is not the only mineral dug out of the ground like this. Iron ore, and another mineral called bauxite, are also strip-mined.

The cutter of a strip mining machine. Its size can be seen from the figure standing near it. People do not usually stand so close!

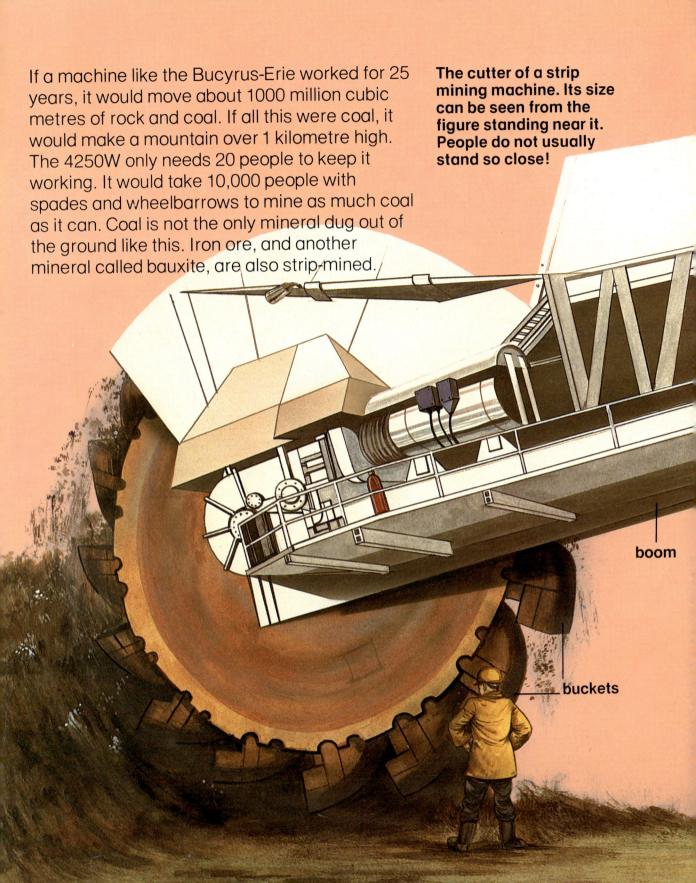

boom

buckets

Oil rig

Oil from under the ground has been used for more than 100 years to give us fuel and chemicals. Cars and the modern chemical industry use a great deal of oil.

When oil was first discovered it was near the surface on dry land, and it was easy to reach. As this oil was used up people looked for oil in other places. They found a great deal under the seas, but this is an extremely difficult place to drill.

Workmen on an oil rig are called roustabouts. Here, they are fixing an extra length to the drill as it cuts into the seabed near Brazil.

In places where oil is being drilled the sea-bed can be more than 60 metres deep. In places like the North Sea, the waves may be 15 metres high in winter, and the wind can reach speeds of over 160 kilometres per hour.

Five tugs slowly move an oil rig into position. This can only be done when the sea is calm for several days.

Drilling rigs can be made out of large concrete frameworks joining three hollow legs. Tugs tow the rig into position, then pumps fill the legs with water to sink the rig over the rock where the oil has been found.

Some rigs are over 300 metres from top to bottom, and carry not just the drilling equipment, but a helicopter deck and living quarters for up to 75 people. When they discover oil, they move the rig to drill elsewhere, and install a smaller production platform. This platform draws the oil which has been discovered out of the sea-bed. Then the oil travels through pipes to the shore.

Combine harvester

We usually make flour from wheat. To make the flour, we cut the wheat, thresh the ears to get the grains, and finally grind the grains to produce the flour.

Before powered machines had been invented, all this took a great deal of time and skill. People cut the wheat, gathered it together in bundles, and then beat it to separate the wheat from the stalks. They did all this by hand. A combine harvester does all this work to produce grain ready for grinding.

First it bends all the wheat in the same direction, then it cuts it off like a giant lawn mower. The grain is then threshed, which means that it is shaken so hard that the grains are removed from the stalks.

A blast of air separates the grain from the chaff. Chaff is the outer layer of the grain and the straw. Finally the grain is put into a tank, and the straw is thrown away down a chute at the back.

One person can operate a combine harvester but you need a second person to drive the grain to the storage tank. It can harvest a field as fast as a team of 200 people with horses pulling machinery. Many people who used to work on farms are no longer needed there because machines can do the work more quickly.

Harvesting by hand. From the top: cutting the crop, tying it into bundles, and threshing. It takes a lot of people, and a lot of time, to do all this.

'Combine harvesting' a field of barley. A tractor is moving the grain away. The cut fields make patterns on the landscape.

A combine harvester is a complicated machine powered by a single diesel engine. Can you see all the different parts which move?

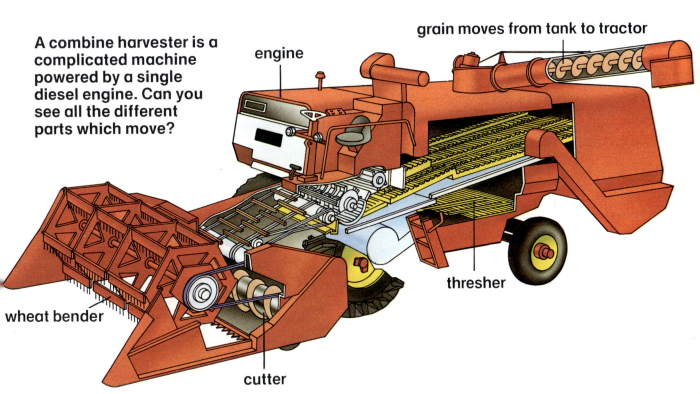

engine

grain moves from tank to tractor

thresher

wheat bender

cutter

Factory ship

People have caught and eaten fish for thousands of years, but not many of us actually catch our own fish before we eat it. It is very difficult to catch enough fish to eat for yourself. It is even more difficult to catch enough to sell in a market. Trawlers and fishing boats travel long distances out to the fishing grounds, to find shoals of thousands of fish to sell in fish markets.

Some factory ships process whales. They are brought on board at the stern, and then the meat is cut up on the deck.

Trawlers have to carry ice to keep their fish cold and fresh on the journey back to port. The fish might rot in the trawler without ice. Factory ships not only catch fish, but also have equipment to process and freeze the fish while it is fresh. This makes sure that the fish tastes better when we eat it. Factory ships can catch and process several hundred tonnes of fish every day.

The 'mother' ship which does the processing is much bigger than the catcher ships which hunt the whales. Most countries have agreed to catch only limited numbers of whales.

The size and efficiency of modern fishing boats has led to problems. For years, more fish were caught than were born to grow up into adults. This is called overfishing, which means taking fish out of the sea faster than they can be replaced. If this went on, the kinds of fish which we eat could almost disappear. To stop this happening, different countries in the world have agreed to catch only limited numbers of fish.

This Sudanese fisherman in East Africa throws his net in a way which has not changed for thousands of years.

MAKING

Tower crane

The last group of machines is the 'making' group. These are machines which help in factories and industries. Cranes make building much easier. They lift materials like bricks and girders to the top of partly-finished buildings.

People use cranes a great deal because they are easy to put up. All the parts are delivered to a building site by lorries. First, the bottom or base is constructed, then the lifting arm and counterweight are put on the base. The vertical part of the crane is built so that it can be pushed up from the middle. This means that the crane can be made taller as the building gets bigger.

Such a crane can be 100 metres high, and can lift a load of 4 tonnes. The counterweight prevents the crane from falling over. The crane operator sits in a cabin high above the building site, and talks to the workers below by radio. Imagine having to climb a 100 metre ladder before starting work each morning!

The operator has controls for turning, lifting, dropping, moving in and out, and operating the grab, the part of the crane which holds the load. The grab can be replaced by a hook, a cement bucket, or other special fittings.

This crane is powered by winches on the ground. There are separate cables to control the in and out movements, as well as up and down.

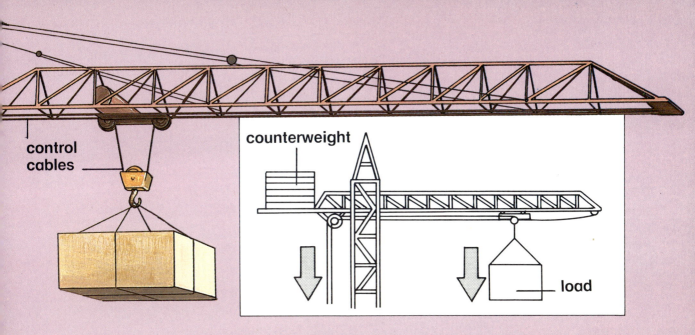

control
cables

counterweight

load

Counterweights are designed to balance the heavy
loads on cranes.

Many cranes can be used on one site. The
operators have to take care that their cranes do not
collide! All these cranes are helping to build a
power station.

Forging metal

Tools such as knives, forks and scissors are all made of steel, which must be hammered into shape. That work used to be done by hand. Blacksmiths heated the metal red hot to soften it, and then hammered it to the right shape.

Their workshop was called a forge. Large modern forges are not powered by people's muscles, but by steam, water or electricity. Otherwise they work in much the same way: by heating metal to soften it, and then hammering it. Large forges like these are faster, more accurate, and much larger than the ones village blacksmiths used.

As engineers designed bigger and better machines, they needed larger and larger forges to shape the metal pieces which the machines are made from.

An ingot of steel is being lifted towards the forge by the heavy chains around it. Hammering it into shape will take several hours.

Modern forges can apply a force of 100 tonnes. This is the same as the weight of about 100 cars, or 1500 people. They are used to shape huge ingots of metal which will be used as parts of other super machines.

First, the steel is heated red hot in a furnace and then placed in the forge. The hammer is slowly lifted by water pressure, and then allowed to fall with an enormous crash, which makes the ground shake. As the hammer lands, it forces the metal into the right shape.

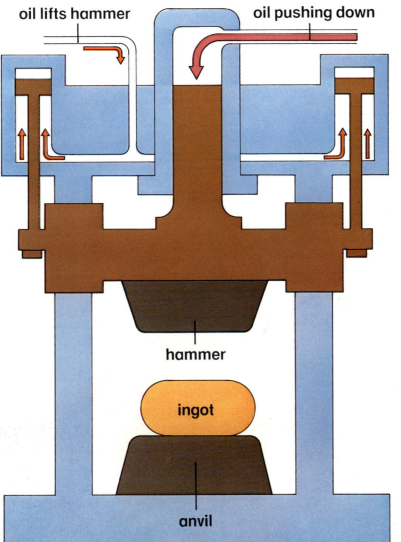

oil lifts hammer

oil pushing down

hammer

ingot

anvil

Oil at high pressure is forced into the side pipes to lift the hammer. This oil is then released and the hammer begins to fall. At the same time more oil is forced into the centre pipe, pushing the hammer even harder.

Beam engine

It is easy to forget that there were super machines in earlier centuries. For example, a Cornish beam engine was used from 1846 to 1943 to pump drinking water for the city of London. Not many machines built today will still be working a century from now. This engine is now in a museum but still works perfectly, and runs once a week for visitors.

The main steam cylinder is 3 metres in diameter and 6 metres tall. The beam is 12 metres long and weighs over 40 tonnes. The engine shed has three levels, and is 25 metres high all together.

To save time, the engineer used to have to crawl along this beam while it was moving to put lubricating oil into the pistons.

Each stroke of the pump takes about 10 seconds and could pump up to 400 gallons into the storage tank at the top of a water tower. People stopped using this type of engine when more efficient engines, called rotary engines, were introduced.

Although it was not as efficient as the newer machines, the beam engine was not worth replacing, as it still worked perfectly. In the end, the need for drinking water grew so much that the beam engine could not pump the water fast enough.It was replaced by more powerful diesel engines and pumps. Both the engines and the pumps fit in a room only one twentieth of the size of the beam engine shed.

The steam cylinder on the right is controlled by the man operating the valves. Steam is used to force down the piston on the right. Then the counterweight on the left pulls the piston up again.

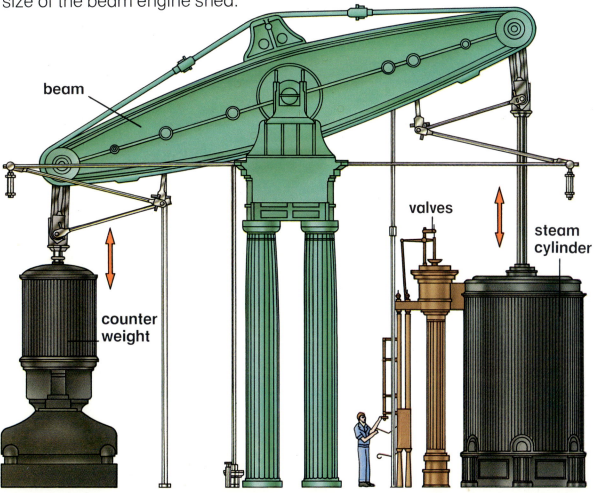

beam

counter weight

valves

steam cylinder

GLOSSARY, BOOKS TO READ

A glossary is a word list. This one explains unusual words that are used in this book.

Bauxite A mineral which looks like clay. Factories melt it and pass electricity through it to make aluminium.

Blacksmith A village blacksmith did all the metal work for a village. He put iron shoes on horses, made farm tools and pots and pans.

Caterpillar tracks Tracks used instead of tyres on vehicles such as bulldozers. Tracks can travel over ground which wheels with tyres would not go over.

Concrete This is a mixture of cement, gravel, sand and water. It sets to a hard solid, and is used in roads and buildings.

Cylinder The smooth tube in which a piston moves.

Factory A factory is a place where things are made, usually in large amounts.

Forge A place where metal is shaped.

Ingot A piece of metal which has not yet been hammered into a useful shape.

Lighthouse This is a building with a light on the top to warn ships of rocks and reefs.

Locomotives The engines of railway trains, powered by steam, diesel or electricity.

Lubrication Adding oil or grease to machinery so that the parts move smoothly.

Pantograph Part of a train which collects electricity from wires above a railway line. It can move up and down.

Piston This is forced up and down a cylinder by steam, gas, or liquid and often moves a wheel.

Propeller A turning shaft with blades which drives some aeroplanes and ships.

Rotary engine An engine that moves round rather than up and down. It uses less fuel and has fewer moving parts than a beam engine.

Trawler This is a fishing boat that drags a large net behind it, scooping up fish.

BOOKS TO READ

How Machines Work by Christopher Rawson, Usborne 1976

Finding out about Science: Engines by Paul Roberson, Hart Davis Educational 1975

Space Flight by Stewart Cowley, Piccolo 1981

Farm Worker and **Car Worker** by Sarah Cox and Robert Golden, Kestrel Books 1975

Aeroplanes by Denis Sheahan, Black 1982

Railways by David Crystal and John Foster, Edward Arnold 1979.

Tools by Robin Kerrod, Franklin Watts 1977

Mechanics by J. Freeman and M. Hollins, Macdonald 1983.